Tales the Elders Told

Tales the Elders Told
Ojibway Legends

Basil H. Johnston

Paintings and drawings by
Shirley Cheechoo

RŌM
Royal Ontario Museum

ISBN 0-88854-261-5

Canadian Cataloguing in Publication Data
   Johnston, Basil H., 1929-
      Tales the elders told

ISBN 0-88854-261-5 (bound)

1. Ojibwa Indians — Legends.* 2. Indians of
North America — Legends. I. Royal Ontario Museum.
II. Title.

E99.C6J624   398.2097   C81-094102-3

ACKNOWLEDGEMENTS

I wish to thank the elders of the Ojibway peoples for these stories and particularly Wahwahskgone for her permission to include *The first butterflies, How bats came to be,* and *Thunderbirds and fireflies* in this collection. My thanks go also to Mrs. Pat Urquhart for typing the stories.

The Legends

Mother, we will never leave you   9

The first butterflies   12

Why birds go south in winter   17

How bats came to be   26

How spiders came to be   31

How dogs came to be   36

Thunderbirds and fireflies   40

The "close your eyes" dance   46

Waugoosh and Myeengun   56

Introduction

Each of the four sons of Winona and Epingishimook (West Wind) left special gifts to the Anishinaubeg (Ojibway). From Mudjeekawiss came courage and a heritage; from Papeekawiss, a sense of beauty and ceremonies; from Chibiabos, romance and poetry; and from Nanabush, humour and the art of story-telling.

It is through stories that the knowledge and understanding of one generation are passed on to the next. Although the themes are far-ranging and often deep and serious, the story-tellers could always relate the stories with humour. If the humour that forms an essential part of Indian story-telling is not present in this small collection, the lack may be attributed not to any lack of skill on the part of the story-tellers but to translation and the limitations of the printed word. Still, if these stories do no more than give some idea of the scope of the Ojibway imagination, and perhaps bring a smile, they will have fulfilled their purpose.

Mother, we will never leave you

After the earth was made, there were only trees, grasses, and flowers upon it. There were no birds, no animals, no insects. On the whole earth there was only one living being—Spirit Woman.

For a long time Spirit Woman was content to live alone. She made mats and baskets and twines. She picked berries and fruits. She made clothes for herself. She was always very busy.

But after living alone for many years, Spirit Woman began to long for a friend. The more she thought about a friend, the lonelier she became. At last the Great Spirit, Kitche Manitou, sent her a husband to ease her loneliness. The two were very happy together.

It was not long before Spirit Woman gave birth—first to a ruffed grouse. On the same day she gave birth, one by one, to all the birds that inhabit the earth and fly in the sky. But only the ruffed grouse stayed with her. Soon after they were born, all the other birds flew away. Spirit Woman was sad when they left her.

"I will never leave you, Mother," promised the ruffed grouse. "I will always be near you, no matter where you are." Spirit Woman appreciated the loyalty of the ruffed grouse and was kind and gentle to the bird.

On another day Spirit Woman gave birth a second time—first to a rabbit and then one by one to all the other animals. This time only the rabbit stayed to comfort her mother. All the other creatures—the bear, the moose, the lynx, the mouse, and all the rest—fled as soon as they could.

"I will never leave you, Mother," promised the rabbit. "I will always stay close to your side."

Because the rabbit was so devoted, Spirit Woman gave the little creature a gentle nature. Because the rabbit was so loyal, Spirit Woman created a rock in the form of a rabbit in the place where she had given birth. In later years people called the rock "The Sitting Rabbit".

Then Spirit Woman gave birth a third time—this time near the sea. One by one, Spirit Woman brought forth all the water creatures, beginning with the whitefish. The whitefish was the only one that stayed to look after Spirit Woman. All the other fish soon deserted their mother.

Even though Spirit Woman had reason to be sad when all the creatures left her, she found contentment with the ruffed grouse, the rabbit, and the whitefish. They always stayed close to her.

The first butterflies

Long ago, when human twins were born to Spirit Woman, she relied on the animals to help her take care of them. All the animals loved the first human babies and did everything they could to help them.

The dog watched over them. The bear gave his fur to keep them warm. The wolf hunted for them. The doe provided them with milk. The beaver and the muskrat bathed them. The birds sang lullabies to them.

The dog was an excellent guardian. The twins had only to cry out and the dog jumped to his feet, his tail wagging. When he found out what was troubling the children, he set it right—or called someone else who could help.

Did the babies need fresh moss to keep them comfortable? The dog appealed to the muskrat and the beaver. Were the babies hungry? The dog ran to the wolf, or to the doe who gave the babies her nourishing milk. Were the flies bothering the infants? The dog asked the spider for help—or jumped and snapped at the pests until the babies laughed.

When the babies wanted to be amused, the dog did his best tricks for them. He rolled over, he sat up, he wagged his tail. He tickled the babies into delighted laughter by licking their noses. When the babies were quiet again, the dog sank down beside them and covered his eyes with his paws—to rest until he was needed again.

After a long time, it became clear that something was wrong with the children. The worried animals, who had been summoned by the bear, gathered round the twins.

"Brothers," said the bear, "the children cannot walk. They do not run and play as our young do. What can we do to help them?"

The wolf spoke first. "They eat the meat I bring them. They are not weak."

The doe agreed. "Every day they drink milk."

The beaver and the muskrat told the other animals that the twins waved their arms and legs with great strength at bath time. Indeed, they often splashed and splashed until the beaver and the muskrat were soaked and out of patience. Then the twins laughed as if they understood what they had done. They went on waving their arms and legs as the fish had taught them to do.

When Nanabush came to play with the children, the animals told him of their concern. Nanabush thought awhile and then he said, "You have cared for the children very well. In fact, you have cared for them so well that they never need to do anything for themselves. All little ones need to reach out for what they want instead of always having everything handed to them. I shall find out what we can do to help the babies learn to walk."

Nanabush journeyed far to the west, to the land of high mountains, where the cloudy peaks stretch up to the sky. From the towering heights, he called to the Great Spirit who was the creator of the children and had been watching over them. The Great Spirit would know what should be done to teach the children to walk.

In reply to Nanabush's call, the Great Spirit told him to search along the slopes of the mountains. There he would find thousands of tiny sparkling stones. Nanabush did as the Great Spirit had said. He collected hundreds of stones—blue ones and green ones and red ones and yellow ones. Soon he had a huge pile that gleamed through the clouds.

Nanabush squatted beside the pile of coloured stones and watched them for a long while—but nothing happened. At last Nanabush grew bored and restless and began to toss the stones, one after another, into the air. As the stones fell back to earth, he caught them.

Then he tossed a handful of stones into the air, catching them as they fell back. He threw a second handful, but this time nothing dropped back into his outstretched hands. Nanabush looked up. To his astonishment, he saw the pebbles changing into winged creatures of many colours and shapes.

The beautiful creatures fluttered here and there before they came to nestle on Nanabush's shoulders. Soon he was surrounded by clouds of shifting colours. And these were the first butterflies.

The butterflies followed Nanabush back to the twins, who crowed with pleasure and waved their legs and stretched out their arms to the beautiful creatures. But the butterflies always fluttered just beyond the grasp of the small outstretched hands. Soon the twins began to crawl, and then to walk, and even to run in their efforts to catch the butterflies.

(Wahwahskgone)

Why birds go south in winter

Long ago there was only summer. The days were always warm and sunny. Winter and snow were unknown.

For the young it was a time of happiness. They played all the time. Animals played with animals. Fish played with fish. Insects played with insects. Birds played with birds. They had many games—hide-and-seek, blind-man's buff, and tag. They ran races, they wrestled, and they played lacrosse. The lakes, the meadows, and the skies rang with their laughter.

From dawn to dusk the young played. No sooner had they finished one game than they began another. They ate little and rested even less. For the parents it was a time of worry. All they could do was try to keep their offspring from harming themselves. Only nighttime brought rest.

Mong, the loon, was no different from any of the other young birds. He played all their games. But most of all he liked to play lacrosse. If he had had his way, he would never have played anything else. The trouble was that his friends did not always want to play lacrosse. Sometimes Mong had to beg them to share his game. When they agreed, and that was not often enough, he was happy. When they refused, he was sad. Mong simply had to find a way to make his friends play lacrosse with him whenever he wanted.

Finally Mong decided that the only thing to do was to challenge the other birds to a match. Off he went to look for someone to challenge. He did not have to go far.

Almost at once he met the raven. Boldly Mong dared him, "My team can beat the feathers off your team any time." The raven cackled and croaked and then flew off without bothering to answer Mong.

Mong watched the raven disappear. He was very upset that the raven had paid no attention to his dare. Oh well, he thought to himself, there are better players than the raven. Besides, the raven cheats. Deep in thought, Mong almost bumped into Benae, the grouse.

Once again Mong tried a bold challenge. Looking Benae in the eye, he snarled, "Get out of my way, runt, or I'll rub your beak in the ground—just as I would on the lacrosse field."

Benae puffed up his feathers in anger. Then just as quickly he relaxed and a smile spread slowly over his face. "I know what you're up to," Benae said, "but you can't trick me. I don't feel like playing lacrosse. Get somebody else." And Benae turned and strutted off into the bush.

Mong was stunned. Twice he had been refused—very rudely. Well, he would just have to try again.

Before long Mong spied Kaikaik, the hawk, sitting on a dead tree cleaning his beak. Mong was just about to dare Kaikaik when he remembered his meeting with Benae. This time he spoke very pleasantly.

"Do you want to play lacrosse, Kaikaik?" Mong asked.

"I don't think so," Kaikaik squawked. "It's too hot."

Mong answered very quickly, for he realized that Kaikaik had not said no. "We can play tomorrow," he said, "but let's choose our teams now. You can have first choice."

Kaikaik stretched out his wings and shook his tail. "Lacrosse is no fun when it's so easy for me to win," he said. To show his strength Kaikaik squeezed the dead tree with his talons—so hard that he broke off some chips.

"Let's make a bet then," Mong answered. "If you win, I'll do whatever you want. If I win, you'll have to play lacrosse with me whenever I want."

"You're taking a big chance," Kaikaik said. "I'm sure to win. Then you'll have to do whatever I ask."

"Yes, yes!" Mong replied eagerly. He knew that he would win. "Let's choose our teams now."

First Kaikaik picked the raven, and Mong picked the Canada goose. Then Kaikaik asked for the cardinal and Mong for the kingbird. Next Kaikaik chose the owl and Mong the robin. By the end of the afternoon the teams were made up. On his side Kaikaik had the raven, the owl, the chickadee, the snowbird, the cardinal, the woodpecker, the grouse, the junco, the pheasant, the partridge, the magpie, and the ptarmigan. Mong had the Canada goose, the kingbird, the robin, the sparrow, the bluebird, the oriole, the scarlet tanager, the plover, the thrasher, the swallow, the catbird, and the kingfisher.

Kaikaik's team was strong and included a few cheaters like the

raven, but Mong was not worried. He had the kingbird on his side. The kingbird could handle anyone on Kaikaik's team.

"We'll meet tomorrow morning as soon as the sun comes up," Mong said. "And the team that scores the first goal wins the game."

"Agreed," answered Kaikaik.

The next morning at sunrise all the birds gathered to watch the two teams play. Kaikaik's fans were on one side of the field and Mong's were on the other.

The game started. The woodpecker was keeping goal for Kaikaik's team and the oriole for Mong's. From the beginning Mong's team went on the attack. Their fans cheered loudly. Mong's players were very quick, but they could not seem to score. Still, Kaikaik's fans were quiet. Their team was slow. It seemed to be just a matter of time before Mong's team slipped a goal past the woodpecker.

Soon the grouse was injured and had to leave the field. Mong's supporters cheered. Then the raven was knocked down. He lay on the field rolling in pain and croaking for help. No one paid any attention to him. The rule was that play would not stop until the first goal was scored.

Then the swallow got the ball. He threw it with all his might towards Kaikaik's goal. As the ball went flying past the raven, he jumped to his feet and caught it. Off he raced towards Mong's goal. With a quick flip, he scored on the oriole.

From Mong's fans came a mighty groan. From Kaikaik's fans came an even mightier cheer. Kaikaik led his team to the middle of the field to meet Mong and his players. The fans crowded in to hear what Kaikaik would demand of Mong.

"Mong," Kaikaik said, "this is your penalty for losing. From now on, whenever the east wind blows, it will bring clouds and rain and thunderstorms, and you won't be able to play lacrosse."

The birds gasped. They had never heard of such a thing. But Mong did not pay much attention. "You only won because the raven cheated," he shouted. "We were winning until the raven pretended that he was hurt."

Kaikaik bristled and his eyes blazed. Mong went right on, "Let's have another game tomorrow. I know you can't win without cheating."

"What's the bet?" asked Kaikaik.

"The same bet," said Mong. "If I win, you must play lacrosse whenever I ask you. If I lose, I must do whatever you want. This time, though, I'd like to have the raven on my team."

"Agreed," said Kaikaik. "We can win without him."

At daybreak the next day a huge crowd gathered at the field. Even the animals came to watch. Who would win the second game? What penalty would Kaikaik demand if he won a second time?

Once again, right from the start, Mong and his team carried the play to Kaikaik's end of the field. They passed the ball so quickly and so deftly that Kaikaik's players could not touch it. Still, Mong's team could not score on the woodpecker. He darted this way and that, blocking the ball with his feet, his wings, and his tail. The game went on and on.

Late in the afternoon Mong's team began to tire. One of Kaikaik's players got the ball and threw it down the field towards Mong's goal. The raven, who was playing just as hard for Mong as he had for Kaikaik, caught the ball. He raced towards Kaikaik's goal. As he ran, the grouse came up behind him and tripped him. The raven lost the ball. The grouse grabbed it and carried it back down the field. Just as dusk was falling, he slipped the ball past the oriole and brought the long game to an end.

"Foul, foul!" screamed Mong and his teammates, amid the thundering cheers of Kaikaik's fans. "Foul!" Mong screamed again to Bonsae, the vulture, who was the referee. But Bonsae had not seen the grouse trip the raven. He declared that the score would stand.

Everyone rushed to the centre of the field. What penalty would Mong and his team have to pay this time?

Kaikaik looked sternly at Mong. "From now on," he said, "whenever the north wind blows, it will bring snow and bitter cold. You and your friends will have to leave this land."

That very night the north wind began to blow. Mong and his friends shivered in the snow. They could not stand the cold. Just as Kaikaik had said, they had to leave the land they loved.

Every year after that the north wind brought the cold winter and Mong and his friends had to fly to the south. If Mong had not been so eager to play lacrosse, if he had not made that foolish bet, winter would never have come.

How bats came to be

Early one morning while he was on his way to his home in the sky, Father Sun got caught in the branches of a tall tree. He tried and tried to free himself, but only managed to entangle himself more firmly. Soon Father Sun could not move at all.

That morning all the animals waited in vain for Father Sun. When he did not appear, they went quietly back to their beds. They thought that they had not slept long enough and it was still night. The bear went back to his cave. The rabbit returned to his nest under a bush at the edge of a field of sweet clover. The chipmunk went into his hole in the roots of an oak tree. Only the owl, the wolf, and the fox were happy, for they could hunt a little longer than usual in the dark.

When Father Sun did not appear the next day, the animals began to suspect that he had got lost on the way home. They searched through most of the forest, but they could not find him.

One little squirrel always looked at the treetops because he liked to jump from branch to branch. He discovered Father Sun stuck in the topmost branches of a tall tree. By this time Father Sun was very pale and weak.

"Little squirrel, little squirrel," he rasped in a low voice, "little squirrel, set me free."

"Certainly, Father Sun," replied the little squirrel, and he ran up the trunk of the tree towards the topmost branches. But Father Sun's heat drove him back to the ground at once.

Again Father Sun called out, "Little squirrel, little squirrel, set me free, set me free."

"Oh, Father Sun, you are too hot," said the little squirrel sadly. "You have already burnt my fine long tail." He had always considered his tail very handsome and was sorry that it was gone.

"Try again," pleaded Father Sun. "I am so tired that my light will soon go out."

The little squirrel ran up the trunk of the tree a second time. He almost reached Father Sun before the fierce heat drove him back.

As the squirrel reached the ground once more, Father Sun groaned, "Little squirrel, little squirrel, please try one more time."

"Father Sun," cried the squirrel, "your heat has burnt off my fine long tail. My fur is black. What is more, I can't see. Your light has made me blind."

"Please, little squirrel, try again," whispered Father Sun. "My light will soon go out."

Once more the little squirrel ran up the trunk, this time as fast as he could go. When he reached the branches at the top of the tree, he gave Father Sun a tremendous push. At that moment Father Sun broke free and sailed up towards his home in the heavens.

The squirrel held on to the branches with all his might. The intense heat had made his arms grow longer and his skin stretch out. Now it seemed that he was caught at the top of the tree forever. There was no one that could rescue him. His scorched skin hurt and his eyes were so sore that he could not see at all.

Father Sun paused and looked back. He was distressed to see how much he had harmed the kind squirrel and knew that somehow he must help the little creature.

"Poor little squirrel," he said, "in helping me you have been hurt. Now I shall repay your kindness. What is your dearest wish?"

"I have always wanted to fly," the squirrel answered, "but now it is too late. I am blind and my skin hurts so much that I must surely die."

Father Sun nodded and suddenly the pain left the squirrel. But he still could not see and his skin and arms were still stretched.

"From now on," said Father Sun, "you will be able to fly into the heavens just as you have always wanted to do. Since my light hurts your eyes, you will fly at night. Although your eyes are blind, your ears are still very sharp. When you call out, the trees

and rocks will send back echoes to you. Then you will know that there is something in your way and you will be able to dive and swoop to avoid hurting yourself. I shall see you in the morning and in the evening on my journey back and forth."

The squirrel dropped his arms from the branches and flew away. He had become a little brown bat. Ever afterwards he would hang upside down when he slept in the daytime. Then everyone would remember the day a squirrel saved Father Sun so that the world could have light and warmth.

And that is how a squirrel became a little brown bat.

(Wahwahskgone)

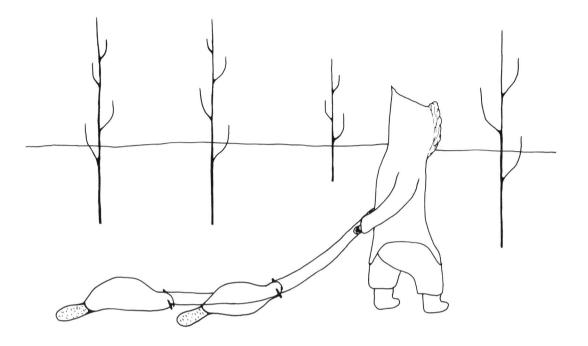

How spiders came to be

Even though there were animals, birds, fishes, fruits, and vegetables in abundance, there was scarcity. In the midst of plenty there was hunger. It seemed that no matter how much game men killed, or how much food women stored away, there was never enough for the next day. For some strange reason that people could not understand, all the food spoiled and turned green.

Hunters killed enough animals, fishes, and birds to feed their families for days—even weeks. The hunters brought home

31

enough food to allow them many days of rest. Yet they had only unending toil.

In vain the people tried to understand this riddle. In vain they tried to keep their food fresh and fit to eat. They hung the flesh of game high up in the trees. Still the flesh turned green and rotted. They buried the meat in the ground. Even in the ground there was no protection. The meat became mouldy and sour. They tried keeping the meat in water, both hot and cold. That worked no better than hanging the flesh or burying it. Nothing, it seemed, could be done to preserve the food, prevent waste, and save labour.

Hunters had to kill many, many creatures to provide enough food. At last the hunting and killing drove the animals from their grounds and greatly reduced their numbers. As food became scarcer, men, women, and children began to grow very sick and to die.

At the same time, life was very hard for a small, six-legged, pot-bellied bug, the Manitoosh. He lived on the juices of the flesh of flies. But he was slow and awkward and could not catch the nimble flies.

The Manitoosh tried every way he could think of to catch the flies. He hid in dark corners and darted out at them. The flies sneered and flew away. He hurled grains of sand at the cunning insects. The flies laughed and flitted out of the way. He tried letting himself down from above by means of a special thread that he made. Again the flies laughed and dodged out of reach.

Finally the Manitoosh and his brothers (the Manitooshug) decided to ask the Great Spirit, Kitche Manitou, for help. They went to a high mountain to plead with Kitche Manitou to make

them better hunters of flies or to make it possible for them to eat other foods.

When the Manitooshug reached the peak, they cried out, "Kitche Manitou, we are hungry and helpless. We come to you for help. Hear us."

Kitche Manitou heard and replied. "What is it that you want?" The Manitooshug asked him for power to catch the flies.

In reply the voice of Kitche Manitou echoed over the mountain top. "I have given you all the power you need. If you use it wisely, it will serve you well." And the voice faded away.

Discouraged, the Manitooshug left the mountain. They would have to go on trying to catch flies.

For a long time no one realized that the troubles of the people and the troubles of the Manitooshug were related. Then the hunters had a great council with a powerful spirit, Nanabush. They wanted to talk about the rotting meat and the vanishing game.

Just before the council there was a great feast. During the meal swarms of flies crawled over the food and the feasters. Many Manitooshug ran and leaped and jumped, trying to catch the flies. But they were just too clumsy.

Nanabush felt sorry for the little creatures and forgot the purpose of the great council. "We must help the Manitooshug," he said to the chiefs and wise men present. "They cannot catch the flies and are very hungry."

Then Nanabush spoke to a Manitoosh. "Brother," he said, "I have watched you trying to catch the flies. I know that you can make a thread to let yourself down from above. Couldn't you use the thread to make a trap for catching flies?"

Although the Manitoosh was doubtful, he hurried home and that same afternoon began to weave the thread in a criss-cross fashion. All afternoon and all evening he worked. When night came, he was very tired and fell into a deep sleep.

It was nearly noon when the Manitoosh awoke the next day. As soon as he opened his eyes, he saw the net of thread he had woven the day before. To his joy and surprise there were two flies trapped in it.

After he had eaten his fill, the Manitoosh rushed off to find Nanabush to tell him about the flies he had trapped. Then he told the other Manitooshug about his discovery. And he taught them how to make nets.

From that day on the Manitooshug made nets and caught flies and ate well. From that day on people were able to keep meat fresh a little longer. And from the Manitooshug they learned how to make nets to catch fish.

Because the Manitooshug had helped the people, Kitche Manitou gave each bug an extra pair of legs. He also gave the bug a new name, Supp-Kay-Shee or Net-Maker.

All this happened before people knew how to preserve meat and other foods.

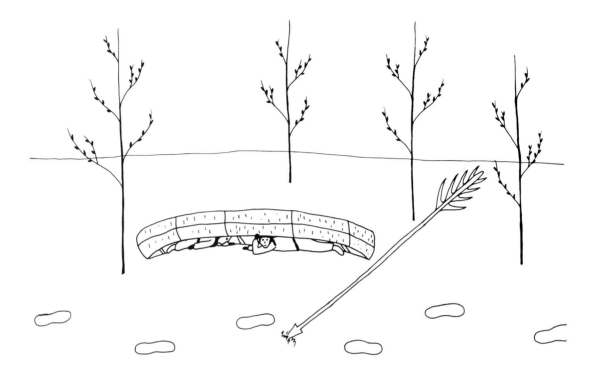

How dogs came to be

One day two fishermen were paddling home along the shore when a violent wind came up and blew them far out to sea. At last they reached the opposite shore. There they found the footprints of some enormous creature. The two men were terrified. They carried their canoe into the forest, turned it upside down, and hid under it.

While they lay shivering with fear and wondering what to do, they heard a crash and felt the earth tremble. Peering out from under their canoe, they saw a huge arrow embedded in the soil not far from them. At the same moment they felt the earth quiver once more.

Then they heard a deep voice saying, "Neekaunssidog (brothers), don't be afraid. I am Giant. I will not harm you."

Still very frightened, the fishermen crawled out from under the canoe. There before their eyes was Giant, with a caribou hanging from his belt. The two men guessed that he had been hunting.

Because Giant seemed harmless and kind, the two fishermen agreed to go home with him. Giant picked them up, put them in his medicine bundle, and carried them off. When they arrived at his home, Giant took the men out of his pouch and put them in a quill box—warning them to be very quiet.

Soon they heard someone come into the lodge. "There are people here," the newcomer growled.

"Windigo, there is no one here," Giant replied.

"Yes, yes, there are people here," Windigo insisted.

"There is no one here," Giant repeated. "If you don't keep quiet, I'll have to throw you out."

"We've told you not to bring people to our land. I'm going to search," Windigo said.

"Windigo," growled Giant, "this is my home. I can bring anyone I choose here, but there is no one."

"I don't believe you and I'm going to search," Windigo answered.

"Windigo, if you don't leave right away, I'll set my guard on you," Giant threatened. Windigo paid no attention to Giant and went right on searching.

Through the chinks in the quill box, the two fishermen could see Windigo searching everywhere. He was even bigger than Giant. Then they saw Giant lift a wooden bowl that was lying upside down at his feet. From under the bowl came a strange four-legged creature. The fishermen had never before seen anything like him.

Giant pointed to Windigo and commanded his pet, "Get him!" The little animal growled and breathed in deeply. With each breath he grew larger, until he was huge. The dog, for that is what the creature was, growled and bared his fangs. Windigo ran out of the lodge, with the snarling dog at his heels.

Giant and the two fishermen could hear groaning and growling and the sounds of struggling and fierce fighting. Then there was silence. At last the dog came back into the lodge—still panting hard.

Earlier the dog had grown huge by breathing in. Now he began to grow smaller as he breathed out. Before long he was the size of an ordinary dog. The two fishermen were astonished.

Sensing their fear, Giant spoke to them. "My brothers," he said, "don't worry. Windigo is gone. I won't hurt you. I just wanted to see what you were like. You may go home now. Since you have come a long way and have a long way to go back, my dog will keep you company on the journey and protect you."

Then Giant said to his pet, "Go with these men. Take them home. Watch over them."

The dog seemed to understand and wagged his tail. Once again he breathed in deeply so that he would grow bigger. When the dog was very large, Giant placed the two fishermen on his back and bade them farewell.

The dog set out across the great sea. He was so tall that the water scarcely reached his back. It did not take him long to cross the sea. On the opposite shore the dog began to breathe out in gasps. As he did so, he shrank little by little until he was no bigger than a fox. Then off he ran into the forest, much to the disappointment of the two fishermen.

When the men reached home, there was the dog happily wagging his tail, barking, and jumping up to lick their hands. And that is the way it has been between man and dog ever since. The dog is happy to be with his master, sad to see him leave, glad to see him return.

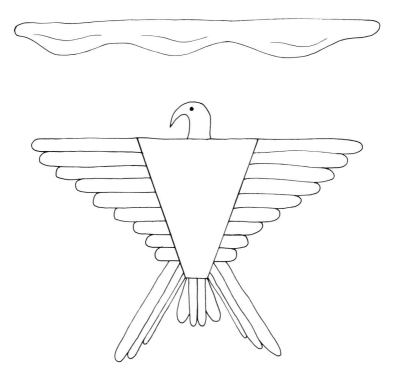

Thunderbirds and fireflies

Thunderbirds are not like other birds. Oh, to be sure, they have feathers—but they are feathers that shine with many, many colours too bright for the human eye to see. Nor do thunderbirds sing like songbirds. Their song rumbles and echoes from cloud to cloud until it becomes a booming mountain of sound that shakes the ground below. What is more, lightning flashes from the eyes of thunderbirds in fiery orange chains or in glowing sheets.

Yet in autumn when the cold sets in and the drumming rains dull the bright leaves, the thunderbirds fly south to the sunny skies just as other birds do. They take the autumn storms with them. Indeed the playful young thunderbirds like to cause wild, noisy storms.

When the thunderbirds return in spring, long before the first robin, the storms that follow them are milder. Last year's mischievous nestlings are older now and less playful. They think only about building their own nests in the northern sky.

One spring when the world was young, all the thunderbirds flew north as usual. In their nesting grounds they shaped their nests from scraps of clouds woven around spring ice and sleet and sealed with night mists and late frost. Then the female thunderbirds laid their snowy, gold-flecked eggs on beds of sparkling breast feathers.

Once the females were settled comfortably, the male thunderbirds began to race through the sky. They talked to one another about the south and warm, lazy days in the sun. They talked even more about something strange they had seen on their way north. Their flight had taken them across what would one day be Michigan. There they had seen great eagles dipping their beaks to the earth and producing very powerful whirling winds—much more powerful than any winds the thunderbirds had ever created. The thunderbirds had been awed, and jealous as well. As they talked about the tornadoes, they grew so excited that they created a terrifying thunderstorm.

The females were very upset and rumbled and squawked among themselves. They simply could not leave the eggs they were sitting on. At last, however, their loud and urgent calls

41

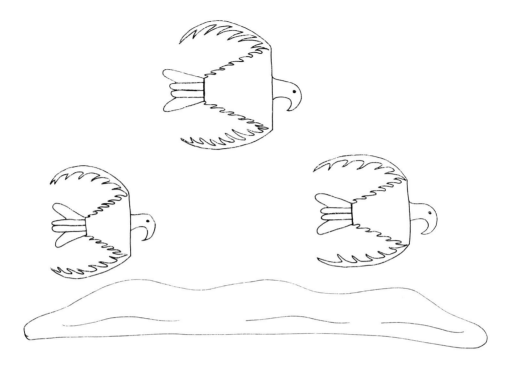

brought the males back to the nests. There the females stroked
their mates' ruffled wing feathers until the males were quiet and
calm again.

Perhaps it was the thunderstorm that caused the young to
hatch early that year, and a noisier, rowdier group of nestlings
had never been seen. They clambered over one another, chirping
in high and noisy bumps of thunder. They demanded food, food,
and more food. Their worried parents flew back and forth, back
and forth, to bring the nestlings all the food they wanted.

When the offspring left the nest—actually they kicked one
another out—the tired parents breathed a sigh of relief. Now that
the little thunderbirds could feed themselves, the parents

expected to be able to relax and enjoy some quiet. But that year they had no time to rest.

No sooner had the little ones taken to the clouds than the fights began. As their parents watched in growing alarm, they fought over wisps of delicious black cloud. When they came to the nests, they battled about positions near their mothers' warm breasts. They tweaked out tail feathers, just to tease. They were always wrestling. The nests were very noisy and very uncomfortable for all the thunderbirds.

Not only were the young birds nuisances at home, but they looked for trouble in the sky. Their favourite trick was to pile cloud upon cloud until the bottoms of the lowest clouds turned into heavy black cumulo-nimbus clouds of great power. Then the

little birds sputtered out rolling grumbles of thunder and their eyes shot out tiny chains of lightning. The clouds tumbled down upon one another until the whole sky was a mottled grey. Then, of course, the naughty birds swooped back to the nests and their parents had to end the storm.

The fathers did not know what to do about their troublesome children. At last they decided to teach them to play lacrosse. They hoped that the young would tire themselves out. Then order could be restored to the sky.

The little thunderbirds learned fast. As you would expect, however, they were careless and thoughtless in their play. Some cut their beaks and others had all their tail feathers pulled out. Still they wanted to play lacrosse. They played from horizon to horizon, from sunrise to dusk, all day, every day.

Their wings grew sore from throwing the big ball their fathers had made for them from the lightning of a tremendous storm. The little thunderbirds did not complain, nor did they rest. They became stronger as they grew older.

Soon the little thunderbirds could throw the ball farther and farther and the game grew more interesting. Although they were strong and quick, they were also very rough. One day a little thunderbird took a mighty sweep and bounced the ball across the goal line, past the line of clouds building up on the horizon, down, far down, to the earth below.

No matter how fast the small thunderbirds chased, swooping and diving, they could not catch it. One of them hurried to the parents for help, but they could do nothing. Before their horrified eyes, the ball plunged to the earth below, crashing with a roar that shook the skies.

The ball scooped out a huge, irregular basin, which we now call Hudson Bay. As the ball broke into pieces, it created all the little lakes in northern Ontario. What a roar of thunder and flash of lightning followed!

There was so much noise and brightness that several stars slipped from their places in the sky. They recovered, hung for a moment, and then fell headlong to the earth below. There they broke into thousands of pieces, which blinked on and off, on and off. The fall had changed the stars into fireflies.

To this day the fireflies can still be seen blinking on and off. People sometimes call them lightning bugs, and so they are, since they were created by thunder and lightning which shook the stars from the sky.   (Wahwahskgone)

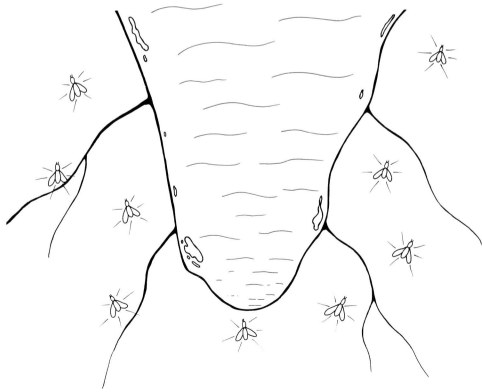

The "close your eyes" dance

Nanabush was very tired. He had walked all day and could go no farther. On the shore of a bay he stopped to drink and splash water on his face. Then he sat down on a large stone beneath a tree to rest his aching bones.

Near the shore on the far side of the bay there was a flock of ducks, swimming and diving and quacking loudly. Their noise drew Nanabush's attention. He squinted in the bright sunlight. Not having eaten all day, Nanabush was hungry as well as tired. The sight of the plump, juicy ducks sent pangs of hunger shooting through his empty stomach.

Nanabush knew there was no point in trying to catch the ducks. They were much too clever. He remembered with shame that once long ago some ducks had tricked him. He had swum underwater to catch them and tie their feet together with a rope so that he could pull them ashore. Instead the ducks had taken flight. Up into the sky they had soared, dragging Nanabush

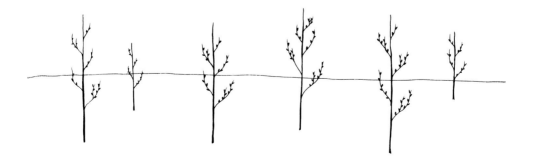

clinging hard to the rope behind them. Weak and frightened and dizzy, Nanabush had lost his grip on the rope and fallen— fortunately for him into the lake. From then on he had always kept away from ducks.

This time, no matter how hard he tried, Nanabush could not ignore the ducks. Their din and clatter carried across the bay. The ducks seemed to be mocking him. There they were eating and playing while he had not a bite to eat and not a single thing to cheer him.

As Nanabush watched the ducks, he began to grow angry. They were fat, and he was thin. They were happy, and he was sad. That did not seem fair. Why should some be well fed while others went hungry, and why should he be the hungry one? His needs were as great as those of others. His skills were equal to those of others. Game was abundant. And yet in the midst of plenty, Nanabush had to go hungry.

To comfort himself, Nanabush took out his drum and began to chant very softly. Almost immediately he began to feel better. Perhaps if he sang, Kitche Manitou would take pity on him. He closed his eyes and chanted a little louder. Then, much more cheerful, Nanabush stood up and began to dance. Perhaps a dance would bring a change in his fortunes.

"Hey, Nanabush!"

Startled, Nanabush shuffled to a halt. One plump little duck had crossed the bay and was now swimming close to Nanabush and looking at him curiously.

"What do you want?" Nanabush demanded.

"What are you doing?" the little duck asked, his eyes wide in wonder.

"Don't you know? I'm chanting and I'm dancing," Nanabush explained.

"May I dance? May I chant?" the young duck asked.

Nanabush laughed. "You! Dance!"

"But I want to dance," the little duck pleaded.

"Your feet are flat! They look like snowshoes," answered Nanabush.

"But I can run on top of water," the duck said.

"That's different," Nanabush answered. "Besides, you're too bow-legged."

"But I want to dance," the little duck begged.

Nanabush felt sorry for the little duck and he forgot about his hunger. "Well, if you want to," he said.

The little duck clambered out of the water. He slipped and slid and waddled over the stones. Even when he was standing, he went on wobbling.

"What do I do?" asked the duck.

"Just do what I do," answered Nanabush, and he began to drum and chant and dance. The little duck—wings outspread, beak open, feet scrunched—tripped and waddled behind Nanabush as if he were walking on hot coals. But all the while he quacked happily.

"Hey, Nanabush, may I dance too?" came another eager voice.

"If you want to," Nanabush muttered. And another duck joined the dance.

For Nanabush, chanting and dancing were forms of prayer. For the ducks, dancing was play and fun. Nanabush was sober and serious, but the ducks quacked and squawked in laughter.

"Hey, Nanabush, may we dance too?" came a chorus of voices.

All the ducks had swum over to the shore where Nanabush was.
Nanabush stopped his chanting and dancing. An idea had just
come to him.

"If you want to," he said. With a glint in his eye, he added, "I
will teach you a new dance. It's called the 'close your eyes'
dance."

All the young ducks cheered and flapped their wings, but one
old duck grumbled, "I have never heard of that dance. How does
it go?"

"It's easy," Nanabush explained, "one long gliding stride and two taps with the foot, one long gliding stride and two taps with the other foot, followed by a wiggle of the tail. You must close your eyes and chant as loud as you can. You must not peek. If you do, the dance is over."

"Good! Good! Good!" the ducks quacked.

Then Nanabush said, "We need a big fire for this dance. Before we begin, you must gather lots of wood."

The ducks did not need to be told twice. They wanted to dance. Off they went—some into the bush, others along the beach. They brought back twigs, branches, and dead wood. Soon there was a huge pile of wood on the beach, enough for a great bonfire.

Nanabush lit the pile of wood. "First, I want you to learn the step," he said. "I will drum and chant. When you have learned the step and the beat, you can chant with me. Chant as loud as you want to, but remember you must not open your eyes. Do you understand?"

"Yes, yes," answered the ducks.

"Make a big circle," Nanabush ordered. And the ducks formed a great circle around the sizzling fire.

Nanabush began to chant. "Aaaayee, eeeeyae." The ducks waddled one long stride and two taps. They were very wobbly.

"Shorten your strides. Your legs are too short and too far apart," Nanabush commanded. After a couple of turns around the fire, Nanabush declared that they were ready to perform the dance.

"Remember," Nanabush said, "I chant and I drum. You chant with me, but keep your eyes closed. Are you ready?"

"Ready," came the reply.

Nanabush began to chant and drum. Soon the ducks were making such a din that Nanabush's voice was drowned out. Only the drum could be heard—and the scraping of feet.

Without losing a beat, Nanabush grabbed a duck, twisted his neck, and tossed him into the fire. The ducks had their eyes closed tight and did not see what was happening. Nanabush seized a second duck and then a third. The dancing and the squawking continued. Nanabush went on seizing ducks, one after another. The other ducks went right on quacking, and dancing, not daring to open their eyes, not wanting to spoil the dance by breaking the rule.

But the old duck was uneasy and opened one eye. To his horror, he saw Nanabush seize a duck, twist his neck, and stuff him into the embers.

"Nanabush is killing us. Fly! Fly! Fly!" the old duck screeched, and he flew off. The other ducks opened their eyes. When they saw what Nanabush was doing, they too flew off, squawking in terror.

Nanabush did not care. He had eight or nine fat ducks. He could not remember how many. As soon as they were cooked, he would eat. He laughed at how clever he had been—tricking the ducks who always had been so watchful.

Still laughing, Nanabush drew in a whiff of the roasting duck. He was hungry, hungrier than he had ever been, and he was tired. All the drumming and chanting and dancing had worn him out. He lay down to rest while the ducks cooked, and soon he was fast asleep.

As Nanabush slept, he began to dream about food, all kinds of food, but particularly roast duck. His dream was so real that he could even smell it.

He awoke with a start. He was no longer tired but he was starving. He rushed to the fire with a picture in his mind of sixteen beautiful drumsticks. With his mouth watering and his stomach telling him to hurry, hurry, Nanabush reached into the fire for the nearest duck.

But all he got was a handful of charred, black bones! While he had slept, the ducks had burnt to a crisp.

Overhead the ducks were screeching. "Have a feast, Nanabush. Shall we have another dance? Will you drum and chant for us while we dance the 'dance of hunger'?"

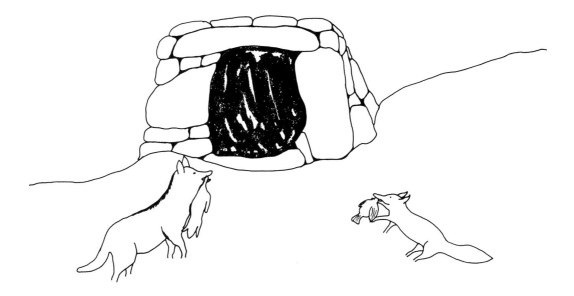

Waugoosh and Myeengun

Long, long ago, all the animals were friends. They looked on one another as brothers. In those days different animals sometimes shared the same den, or cave, or nest.

Among the animals that chose to live in the same shelter were Waugoosh, the fox, and Myeengun, the wolf. They had been friends since they were infants. They not only shared the same den, but they sometimes hunted together and shared their catch. Usually, though, each one hunted alone, chasing the game he liked best. They had found that if they hunted separately, each one in his own large territory, their chances of catching game were better.

Winters then, as now, were hard, with deep snows, chilling cold, and blinding blizzards. Hunting, even for the best hunters like Waugoosh and Myeengun, seldom brought any reward. The most the animals could hope for was just to stay alive through the winter.

One winter was the most severe that Waugoosh and Myeengun could remember. The snow was deeper than ever before, the cold was more biting, and the blizzards lasted longer. Hunting was hopeless. At last Waugoosh and Myeengun were so desperate that they had to eat the bark from the trees. At this rate they would not live many more days, let alone the whole winter.

Still, they went out hunting whenever they could. They did not expect to catch anything, but they wanted to get away from each other. Already they were snarling and quarrelling over little, silly things—something they had never done before.

One clear morning, after a long storm, Waugoosh and Myeengun set out to hunt. They parted at the entrance of their den. Waugoosh made his way very slowly. He stopped often to listen and to peer into clumps of bushes for either rabbits or partridges. But there was nothing to be seen. Early in the afternoon Waugoosh went well beyond his usual hunting grounds.

Since he did not know the area, Waugoosh had to stop often to mark his trail. He had to be sure he would be able to find his way back. All the while he looked around—first on the ground and then upward into the trees. Once his heart leaped. There, sitting on a branch, was a partridge.

Keeping his eyes on the partridge, Waugoosh crept forward. Not until he heard a squeal of fright did he notice a rabbit. He had

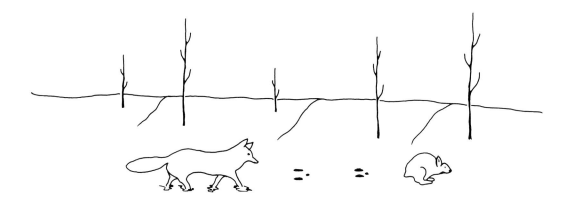

nearly stumbled on the little creature, who was bounding away in
terror. Waugoosh forgot the partridge and began to chase the
rabbit. With his long, swift strides, Waugoosh soon caught up to
his prey. Then just as he was about to pounce on it, the rabbit
changed course. Waugoosh turned sharply, throwing up sprays
of snow. For a few moments the two raced back and forth on the
snow, around the trees and through the underbrush.

But hunger had weakened Waugoosh. Soon he was panting
hard and had to stop running. Very disappointed, he watched the
rabbit disappear into the underbrush. Then he lay down in a
thicket and almost at once he fell asleep.

It was dusk when he awakened with a start, his senses alert.
Crunch, crunch—the sound of snowshoes. Squeak, squeak—
the sound of something sliding on the snow. Waugoosh raised
his head, but it was hard to see through the thicket.

Then Waugoosh spied a shape. It was a man, hunched forward
and pulling a toboggan. Waugoosh watched as the man
disappeared into the shadows of the forest.

Suddenly Waugoosh grew rigid, his nose tingling. What was that smell? He sniffed the air again and rose to his feet. Faint but unmistakable it came to him—the smell of fish!

Food! A meal! Not my favourite meal, thought Waugoosh, but something to keep me, and Myeengun too, from starving.

Silently Waugoosh set off in pursuit and soon caught up to the toboggan. It was loaded with fish, all piled neatly like sticks of wood. The smell almost choked him.

Waugoosh darted forward without a sound. He grabbed a fish from the pile and sped away. No trouble at all, he thought, and the man will never miss one fish. Waugoosh was so pleased with himself that he loped all the way home without stopping.

"Food, my friend! Food!" he shouted as he entered the den. Then tearing the fish in two, he gave half to Myeengun.

Eyes wide in astonishment, Myeengun could only sputter, "Fish. Ugh."

"Eat it and don't think about it," Waugoosh urged.

"You're right," Myeengun answered. "I shouldn't complain, but I hate the smell of fish, and it has so many bones." As he grumbled, he nibbled at the fish. Then he added, "Where did you get it?"

"From the lake," Waugoosh answered.

Myeengun did not believe his friend, but he knew that there was no point in asking again. Waugoosh liked to keep secrets. He would never tell Myeengun the truth about where the fish had come from. Oh well, the important thing was that they had eaten. Still, Myeengun was very curious.

That night, for the first time in weeks, the two slept soundly, untroubled by pangs of hunger. The next day each one set out as usual for his own hunting grounds.

Waugoosh hunted all day without success. Late in the afternoon, he decided to go back to the place where he had seen the hunter the night before. He hid in the same thicket. Just as it was growing dark, Waugoosh heard the familiar crunch, squeak.

Not until the man with the toboggan had gone past his hiding place did Waugoosh creep out of the thicket. Once again he sped noiselessly after the toboggan. Once again he crept up behind it and grabbed a fish from the pile without being caught.

Myeengun was already at home when Waugoosh returned with his prize. "We eat again," called Waugoosh, and he broke the fish in half and offered a piece to his friend.

"It's unbelievable," Myeengun muttered. "How can anyone be so lucky? Where *did* you get the fish?"

"I've already told you. I went fishing," Waugoosh snapped.

For a while Waugoosh returned each evening with a fish. Myeengun returned each evening empty-handed and he grew very unhappy. Then one evening Waugoosh came back with the leg of a deer. That was more than Myeengun could bear—especially when Waugoosh told him that he had snatched it from some lynxes. Waugoosh is growing more and more deceitful, Myeengun thought to himself. And he finished his meal in silence, not enjoying it at all.

Later, when he was not so cross, Myeengun said to Waugoosh, "You shouldn't have to provide all the food. I'd like to do my share."

"Don't worry. I've just been lucky," Waugoosh answered. "You would share with me if you were the lucky one."

"But I could take my turn," Myeengun insisted. "That's only fair. Just tell me where to go."

Then Waugoosh realized that he could not go on deceiving his friend. He would have to confess. "The truth is," Waugoosh said, "that I didn't get the fish from the lake, nor the deer leg from the lynxes. I've been stealing the food from a hunter."

"All the more reason that I should take my turn," Myeengun replied.

"All right, then," said Waugoosh, "here's what you have to do. Just follow my trail. It's well marked and you can't miss it. It leads to the hiding place where I wait for the hunter, who is always on his way home just about dusk. Let him go by and then sneak up quickly behind the toboggan. The fish and game are loosely piled on it. Grab one piece—that's all we need—and run. The hunter won't even notice."

The next day Myeengun followed the trail to the hiding place. There he settled down in the hollow behind the thicket to wait for the hunter. Soon he heard the crunching of snowshoes and the groaning of the toboggan under its burden.

Once the hunter had passed the thicket, Myeengun slid out of his hiding place and darted forward silently. Moments later he crept up behind the toboggan.

Myeengun clamped his jaws on a big fish and gave a quick tug, but the fish would not budge. Something was holding it down. Myeengun tugged even harder, but still the fish would not budge. Then suddenly he felt a sharp whack across his back—and again a whack and a thump and a whack and a thump.

"Eeeyowh!" Myeengun howled. And again and again came a whack and a thump on his back.

"Eeeyowh! Eeeyowh!" Myeengun howled as he was knocked to the ground, where he lay twisting and turning in great pain.

Then he heard the angry voice of the hunter. "So you're the one who's been stealing my food. I'm going to beat you so hard that you'll never steal again." And the hunter struck Myeengun several times more with a big stick before he went on his way.

Myeengun lay groaning and twisting in the snow. Much later he managed to crawl back to the den, moaning all the way.

As Myeengun entered the den, Waugoosh called to him, "It's about time. What kept you? I'm as hungry as can be."

Myeengun bared his teeth and snarled, "Get out! Get out! And never come back. That's the last time you'll ever deceive me." Astonished, Waugoosh fled, wondering what had come over his friend, but not daring to stay and ask.

And never after that did a wolf and a fox live together in the same den or have anything to do with each other.